LIKEABLE LEADERSHIP

I0622631

Welcome to the first reflection journal in the Likeable Leadership series. The elements presented here are found at various points within the Strength in Nature Leadership series. Thank you for entrusting your thoughts and time with me as you work through your transformation to a Likeable Leader.

Why start with Likeable Leadership? As leaders, we must have followers. People naturally follow leaders they like and trust. Likeable Leadership addresses some of the fundamentals associated with all leadership and management theories. A week of reflection is developed for each topic. Each journal offers 31 days of quotes and writing prompts. Each day includes a spot for three priorities and three gratitude memories. This daily practice helps us de-clutter our mind from worry and anxiety while strengthening our propensity to live a joyful and grateful life. The final page incites you to highlight your favorite activities to carry forward with your leadership journey.

I am humbled that you share your thoughts and time with the following pages. This space is designed for you to write and reflect. For more in-depth readings on these topics, visit the website www.strengthinnature.com If you have questions, please email me at angela.buckley@creativelyefficient.com

Yours in nature,

Angela

If found, please return to:

Name: _____

Address: _____

Phone: _____

Email: _____

Month started _____

TABLE OF CONTENTS

Likeable Leadership Elements

1. HUMILITY

Humility is the art of valuing other people and their opinions, thoughts, and needs without indulging in self-pride.

2. GENEROSITY

Generosity is the spirit and action of freely giving to others. It sometimes refers to the overall spirit of kindness.

3. INTEGRITY

Integrity refers to aligning your actions with your words. Many people consider integrity to be "what you do when no one is looking."

4. CONSISTENCY

Consistency refers to being reliable and repeatable. Actions that are consistent are seen as fair and accurate.

5. FRIENDLINESS

In leadership, "friendly" refers to being beneficial or to serving a helpful purpose. "Friendly" combines with an air of warmth and kindness.

6. POSITIVITY

Leaders create the environment around them. The daily approach brings energy and sees the positive outcome to each challenge and opportunity.

7. AVAILABILITY

Leaders are available and responsive to those around them. Time is an important element of leadership when referring to availability and responsiveness.

8. GOOD LISTENING

Listening is a skill that hears both spoken and unspoken words. A true leader hears the body language, understands context, and asks probing questions to seek understanding.

9. FOCUS

Focused leaders concentrate on a particular aim, not wasting time, effort, or energy on other things. Focused leaders are present and work in the moment.

10. CELEBRATION

Likeable leaders laugh and celebrate successes. They work hard to support the team and they play hard to celebrate the joy of life.

11. HONESTY

Likeable leaders are open and sincere. Their words and actions are free of deceit.

12. AUTHENTICITY

Authentic leaders are human and acknowledge their mistakes.

HOW TO USE THIS JOURNAL

WEEKLY THEME

CIRCLE DAY OF THE WEEK

ENTER DATE

S M T (W) T F S

>> At its essence, humility is a quiet power. You have the internal strength to put others before yourself.

FOOD FOR THOUGHT

DAILY PROMPT

What steps can you take to focus more on others? What struggles or situations make your think of yourself first? Can you improve your mental muscles in these situations?

DAILY THOUGHTS

SCRIBBLES

DOODLES

WHAT ARE TODAY'S...

TOP THREE TO-DO

☐ _____

☐ _____

☐ _____

I'M THANKFUL FOR...

DAILY GRATITUDE

☐ _____

☐ _____

☐ _____

>> At its essence, humility is a quiet power. You have the internal strength to put others before yourself.

What steps can you take to focus more on others? What struggles or situations make you think of yourself first? Can you improve your mental muscles in these situations?

TOP THREE TO-DO

☐ _____
☐ _____
☐ _____

DAILY GRATITUDE

☐ _____
☐ _____
☐ _____

STRENGTH IN NATURE
Leadership Series

HUMILITY

» Humility and kindness are tied together. Think of others before you think of yourself. (Note: "before," not "less.") You can spread kindness by understanding from their perspective.

Recall the last time someone made a kind gesture toward you – a smile, an extra thank-you note. How did you feel? How can you spread kindness?

TOP THREE TO-DO

☐ _____

☐ _____

☐ _____

DAILY GRATITUDE

☐ _____

☐ _____

☐ _____

HUMILITY

>> Humility is a lesson we learn and a skill we practice when things go awry. We must pick ourselves up, dust ourselves off, and learn.

Reflect on the last time things did not go as planned. Did you take time to recognize your role or did you blame others? How can you practice humility in learning to be better prepared the next time something like that occurs?

TOP THREE TO-DO

☐ _____

☐ _____

☐ _____

DAILY GRATITUDE

☐ _____

☐ _____

☐ _____

STRENGTH IN NATURE
Leadership Series

HUMILITY

>> When we make mistakes and acknowledge them, we are practicing humility. As we practice, we grow stronger in our acceptance and understanding of humility.

Of the focus weeks this month, where do you feel strongest? How can you continue to develop this strength?

TOP THREE TO-DO

☐ _____

☐ _____

☐ _____

DAILY GRATITUDE

☐ _____

☐ _____

☐ _____

HUMILITY

S M T W T F S ☐

>> Humility includes giving credit to the team when things go well and taking credit when things do not go as planned.

How do you feel when others take credit for your work? How can you be more generous in giving credit?

TOP THREE TO-DO

☐ _____

☐ _____

☐ _____

DAILY GRATITUDE

☐ _____

☐ _____

☐ _____

STRENGTH IN NATURE
Leadership Series

>> In humility, we seek to add value to others. How can we build them up? How can we help them develop?

Adding value to others requires knowing how they want to be valued. This week, can you identify one person on your team and HOW they WANT to be valued?

TOP THREE TO-DO

☐ _____

☐ _____

☐ _____

DAILY GRATITUDE

☐ _____

☐ _____

☐ _____

HUMILITY

S M T W T F S ☐

>> In addition to adding value, a humble leader actively seeks to develop those around them.

Today, look to one person. What is one seed within them that you can fertilize with support and water with kindness?

TOP THREE TO-DO

☐ _____

☐ _____

☐ _____

DAILY GRATITUDE

☐ _____

☐ _____

☐ _____

STRENGTH IN NATURE
Leadership Series

HUMILITY

>> When fuled by a passion, we practice humility by letting it take the attention instead of us. Where do you want to apply your passion?

When fueled by a passion, we practice humility by letting it take the attention instead of us. Where do you want to apply your passion?

TOP THREE TO-DO

☐ _____

☐ _____

☐ _____

DAILY GRATITUDE

☐ _____

☐ _____

☐ _____

GENEROSITY

S M T W T F S ☐

>> Giving requires that we look outside ourselves and understand our team members' needs and desires. It does not have to be a financial gift. As leaders, time, credit, and acknowledgment are excellent gifts.

What power do you share when you graciously recieve a gift?

TOP THREE TO-DO

☐ _____

☐ _____

☐ _____

DAILY GRATITUDE

☐ _____

☐ _____

☐ _____

STRENGTH IN NATURE
leadership series

 **GENEROSITY**

» Generosity impacts joyfulness in both the giver and the receiver. We grow not only through the act of giving, but the act of receiving.

What is one action you can take to spread joy and generate energy in your team today?

TOP THREE TO-DO

☐ _____

☐ _____

☐ _____

DAILY GRATITUDE

☐ _____

☐ _____

☐ _____

 **GENEROSITY**

S M T W T F S ☐

>> Effective generosity has an element of empathy. In seeking to understand, we are generous with our time and our energy.

How can we focus our generosity efforts and thoughts on the needs of others? Can you identify three needs of your team members?

TOP THREE TO-DO

☐ _____

☐ _____

☐ _____

DAILY GRATITUDE

☐ _____

☐ _____

☐ _____

STRENGTH IN NATURE
Leadership Series

» Generosity of spirit is the practice of understanding the intent of a deed before judging the person.

When was the last time you judged someone's intent? How can you understand their perspective and practice generosity instead of judgment?

TOP THREE TO-DO

☐ _____

☐ _____

☐ _____

DAILY GRATITUDE

☐ _____

☐ _____

☐ _____

>> Generosity must be balanced with self-care and self-awareness. Over-giving is no longer generosity. Leaders understand and model this balance.

Presence and self-awareness in giving are important. Are you giving of your time with kindness and joyfulness? How can you share energy with your team by giving your time joyfully?

TOP THREE TO-DO

- [ ] _____
- [ ] _____
- [ ] _____

DAILY GRATITUDE

- [ ] _____
- [ ] _____
- [ ] _____

STRENGTH IN NATURE
Leadership Series

GENEROSITY

S M T W T F S ☐

>> In gifting, we receive. There is a shared joy in giving and receiving.

During this week of practicing and reflecting on generosity, how have these actions impacted you? Are you realizing a lighter feeling? Have you reduced your emotional burdens as you shared joy with others?

TOP THREE TO-DO

☐ _____

☐ _____

☐ _____

DAILY GRATITUDE

☐ _____

☐ _____

☐ _____

GENEROSITY

S M T W T F S

>> Generosity requires an element of timing. As leaders, we learn to "read" those around us and give when the time is right.

This week has focused on time and talent. What gifts have you been able to share: time, talent, donations? How do you lead with generosity?

TOP THREE TO-DO

☐ _____

☐ _____

☐ _____

DAILY GRATITUDE

☐ _____

☐ _____

☐ _____

STRENGTH IN NATURE
leadership series

S M T W T F S

>> Likeable leaders lead with passion and gather followers through their dedication. As leaders, generalisty comes easily when it is tied to our passion.

Your purpose follows closely with your passion. How do you share passion with your team?

TOP THREE TO-DO

☐ _____

☐ _____

☐ _____

DAILY GRATITUDE

☐ _____

☐ _____

☐ _____

LIKEABLE LEADERSHIP

 **INTEGRITY**

>> **Without honesty, there is no integrity.**

Integrity deals with your internal compass. How truthful are you with yourself?

TOP THREE TO-DO

☐ _____

☐ _____

☐ _____

DAILY GRATITUDE

☐ _____

☐ _____

☐ _____

» Do it. Do it right. Do it when no one is looking.

Elite athletes are willing to practice in the rain and in the dark when others are still sleeping. Elite musicians practice when nobody is listening. What actions will you commit to for the next 30 days to practice integrity?

TOP THREE TO-DO

☐ _____

☐ _____

☐ _____

DAILY GRATITUDE

☐ _____

☐ _____

☐ _____

INTEGRITY

>> Integrity includes elements of compassion and empathy.

Do you recognize the human in each team member? Are you challenged in ranking people based on their professional or financial success? What step can you take to see the humanness in each team member?

TOP THREE TO-DO

☐ _____

☐ _____

☐ _____

DAILY GRATITUDE

☐ _____

☐ _____

☐ _____

STRENGTH IN NATURE

 **INTEGRITY**

» Integrity is acting consistently. Clearly articulating your values helps you act with intent and integrity.

Do your internal thoughts, actions and external postings (i.e. social media) align? What can you do to better align your posts with your values?

TOP THREE TO-DO

☐ _____

☐ _____

☐ _____

DAILY GRATITUDE

☐ _____

☐ _____

☐ _____

INTEGRITY   S M T W T F S ☐

>> Integrity requires courage to follow your moral compass when others disagree.

When was one time that you acted with integrity? Did you take a stand against a bully? Did you tell the truth when you were encouraged to lie? How did this stance make a difference in your life or in the lives of those around you?

TOP THREE TO-DO

☐ _____

☐ _____

☐ _____

DAILY GRATITUDE

☐ _____

☐ _____

☐ _____

STRENGTH IN NATURE
leadership series

INTEGRITY

» Quiet integrity is demonstrated daily through consistency of action.

Can the people around you articulate your values based on your words and deeds?

TOP THREE TO-DO

☐ _____

☐ _____

☐ _____

DAILY GRATITUDE

☐ _____

☐ _____

☐ _____

 **INTEGRITY**

S M T W T F S

>> Assess your own integrity periodically to grow in your leadership roles.

Do you remember the phrase, "knowledge is power"? How can you better understand situations and see different perspectives in order to act with integrity?

TOP THREE TO-DO

☐ _____

☐ _____

☐ _____

DAILY GRATITUDE

☐ _____

☐ _____

☐ _____

STRENGTH IN NATURE
Leadership Series

CONSISTENCY S M T W T F S ☐

>> Consistent, measured progress is more effective than one big push: in sports, in leadership, and in life.

In the previous weeks, we reflected upon humility, generosity, and integrity. Moments of these elements are good. Repeated, demonstrated actions demonstrate consistency. How can you create a habit of leadership success based on humility, generosity, and integrity?

TOP THREE TO-DO

☐ _____
☐ _____
☐ _____

DAILY GRATITUDE

☐ _____
☐ _____
☐ _____

 **CONSISTENCY**   S M T W T F S ☐

>> Chase leadership excellence through consistency.

Can you measure your consistency? Consider one daily action that reflects your leadership to track for 30 days.

TOP THREE TO-DO

☐ _____
☐ _____
☐ _____

DAILY GRATITUDE

☐ _____
☐ _____
☐ _____

STRENGTH IN NATURE
Leadership Series

» Leadership excellence requires us to choose to act daily.

Small goals lead to attainable, consistent habits that result in excellence. How can you demonstrate this to those you are leading?

TOP THREE TO-DO

☐ _____

☐ _____

☐ _____

DAILY GRATITUDE

☐ _____

☐ _____

☐ _____

CONSISTENCY

S M T W T F S ☐

>> Leadership, like planning, requires dedication and repetition. In short, consistency.

Plan. Do. Check. Act. This cycle results in regular improvements. Are you planning leadership activities, following through, and evaluating the outcome?

TOP THREE TO-DO

☐ _____

☐ _____

☐ _____

DAILY GRATITUDE

☐ _____

☐ _____

☐ _____

STRENGTH IN NATURE
leadership Series

CONSISTENCY

S M T W T F S ☐

» Leading requires a direction if you want followers.

We run marathons one step at a time. How are you stringing together small wins that result in amazing accomplishments?

TOP THREE TO-DO

☐ _____

☐ _____

☐ _____

DAILY GRATITUDE

☐ _____

☐ _____

☐ _____

CONSISTENCY   S M T W T F S ☐

>> Consistency is not about perfection. It is about simply refusing to give up.

Obstacles abound when in leadership positions. How do you adopt a consistency mindset to overcome them?

TOP THREE TO-DO

☐ _____

☐ _____

☐ _____

DAILY GRATITUDE

☐ _____

☐ _____

☐ _____

CONSISTENCY   S M T W T F S ☐

>> Consistency occurs when your actions align to your values, even when you don't "feel like it."

When overcoming obstacles, how do you assess your actions to align to your values?

TOP THREE TO-DO

☐ _____

☐ _____

☐ _____

DAILY GRATITUDE

☐ _____

☐ _____

☐ _____

 **CONSISTENCY**

S M T W T F S ☐

>> **Consistency is like a vector – it has direction and magnitude.**

Is your leadership leading you and your team in a consistent direction?
Have you clearly communicated the end goal?

TOP THREE TO-DO

☐ _____

☐ _____

☐ _____

DAILY GRATITUDE

☐ _____

☐ _____

☐ _____

STRENGTH IN NATURE
Leadership Series

Highlights

*What are the **top three concepts** you learned from each element?*

*How will you **carry these habits forward** in your leadership practice?*

HUMILITY   *LEARNED*   *DO*

- ☐ _____ ☐ _____
- ☐ _____ ☐ _____
- ☐ _____ ☐ _____

GENEROSITY

- ☐ _____ ☐ _____
- ☐ _____ ☐ _____
- ☐ _____ ☐ _____

INTEGRITY

- ☐ _____ ☐ _____
- ☐ _____ ☐ _____
- ☐ _____ ☐ _____

CONSISTENCY

- ☐ _____ ☐ _____
- ☐ _____ ☐ _____
- ☐ _____ ☐ _____

Thank You

WHAT COMES NEXT

You have just completed Likeable Leadership, Journal 1. The following two journals continue to guide you on your leadership journey. The themes identified in Likeable Leadership have been around for centuries. Numerous coaches and leaders have spent time lecturing and creating presentations on these topics.

You are now on your own journey to become the best you, become a lifelong learner, and be curious. Curiosity takes many forms: reading (hint: there's more information at our website, www.strengthinnature.com/likeableleadership), asking questions, writing (for yourself and for others), and reflecting. Use your senses and wonder at all the amazing influences you can create for your friends, family, and team members.

Leadership starts from within. These exercises seek to support your journey internally so you can support your leadership goals and aspirations externally. Thank you for allowing me to be a part of your journey. I look forward to hearing from you as you progress in journals 2 and 3.

NOTES

NOTES